unknown millionaire

_____

Jasmin Hajro

unknown millionaire

Jasmin Hajro

© 2018

Cover design by Jasmin Hajro

First english edition

10 may 2021

hello, how are you doing ?

My name is Jasmin Hajro
I am 35 years old,
I live in Doetinchem in the Netherlands.

I sell packages of greetingcards, door to door…
for my own company which is called Hajro.

My company also sells giftmugs
and the books that I have written…

and we donate to 15 charities….

the dutch website of my company is www.hajro.be

the english website is www.hajro-international.webnode.nl

I made those websites myself,
with the website editor,
that the provider offers.
(they are www.webnode.nl and www.mijndomein.nl
in case you want to build your own website, you can go there and create it)

In case you don't know my story,
I'll tell you in a nutshell

I was born in Sarajevo,
Bosnia Hercegovina

I lived in a village with my parents,
called Gora,
5 years after my birth
my parents had another child

a girl, my sister Emina.
My parents both worked…
When I was about 8 years old,
the war started between Bosnia and Serbia and Croatia

We moved a couple of times,
because the enemies came to close….

Eventually when I was 10 years old we fled
the country,
and arrived in the Netherlands,
me my sister and our mother…
My father stayed there to fight in the war.

We lived in a few refugee camps
and eventually got a house in Doetinchem
My father got shot,
and also arrived in the Netherlands,
he barely survived…

When our faily was back together
we lived together for about 1 year,
then
my parents split
and eventually divorced.

I and my sister went to school
and learned the Dutch language.
My mother also learned the Dutch language and started working.

My father went away to live with his sister in Smilde
which is 200 km away from here.

I got into puberty and started drinking alcohol
and using drugs…

I got into trouble with the law, because I had stolen tabacco and punched people in the face.

I went to juvenile jail 3 times,
for 8 months in total.

One day I had used too much drugs
and was completely tripping,
I got into a coma
woke up at the hospital,
the next day….

I stopped using drugs after that…

I got a job as a dishwasher at Landal greenparcs
and worked my way up to cook…
I worked there for 4,5 years…

In 2010 I collapsed from working hard and long hours
and drinking alcohol everyday…

After that I got sober…

In 2011 being sober and clean
I started to have hallucinations
at work…

I thought I was going crazy,
couldn't focus
couldn't sleep anymore
and I started coming in late at the job
and soon got fired,
because I didn't function anymore…

The 10 years after that were difficult financially..
I couldn't find work

or keep work for a longer time

It was a lot of stress, paranoia
and low income

I started a business in 2012
and failed
because I didn't know how to sell and get more clients…

I did manual labor jobs and also delivered newspapers and
advertizing…

In 2015 I got an opportunity to sell packages of greetingcards
I got sales training and went out selling
I started to earn money again…

I worked for a foundation,
then there were some problems with it
and I started my own foundation
the Giveth Life foundation.

Then the cops came and told me
that I could only raise money 2 weeks a year
for the foundation in our township.

Then I founded my 2nd company : Hajro
and continued to sell packages of greetingcards.

I used to buy them in Belgium and resell them,
but a few years ago I decided to design my own
unique greetingcards
and sell those…

and that's still my work , my profession…
Today I sold 5 packages of greetingcards
and earned 25,- euros in profits.

The most that I earned selling was E 768 euros.

Since last years I receive subsidy of 650 euros a month
and my earnings from my company are settled
with the subsidy.
So if I earn 200 euros selling,
I receive 450 euros in subsidy.

I will receive that subsidy for 3 years.

I have also gotten help with my debts
from the municipality Doetinchem, the township
In 2024 , after 3 years I will be debtfree…

I have been writing for years in journals…
somewhere in 2017 or 2018 I decided
to publish my writings
and I wrote a lot of books
since then
You can find them at www.amazon.com/author/jasminhajro

On www.smashwords.com
I give away all my books for free
because of corona crisis

I now have medications for the hallucinations,
and they seldom happen again
when it happens it's very brief…

I still live with my other and I am 35 years old

I am on the waitlist for assisted living
that will take 2 years and after that
I will have to rent a house or appartement
and live independent….

My book : Last 10 years was sold 13 times at
www.mijnmanagementboek.nl

and my book : the Diet 7 times.

At www.smashwords.com
more than 600 people have gotten a book of mine

By now I have sold thousands of packages of greetingcards..

And I have donated hundreds of euros to charities.

I have been honest to you

about everything

Maybe you think : it's quite a story

I am lucky to still be alive
and able to work and to write.

I hope that my books will help a lot of people.

By just working and saving you probably won't get rich or financially independent
(''able to live from your own personal resources'')

I have a system to save and invest your money

Work, have an income
save 10 % every month
and invest one third of your savings into
mutual funds and bonds…
Do it every month and every year
It will take you 30 or 40 years to become
financially independent,
but it's worth it…

On the following pages you will learn
the system and how to use it
step by step

In this book you'll discover & learn:

- There is enough money in the world
- the Pay yourself first rule
- 10% of everything
- the secret of success
- Trend (which is important to you)
- Preparation
- Systematically building it up
- Your result after 10 years
- the 2nd secret of success

Before we begin.....

There should be something here
like : If you want to buy financial
products, you should seek an professional.
Someone who works at a bank or whatever.
And the author is not responsible
for your decisions and money.

Which is bullshit.

Because even though it's a nice way
to prevent yourself from being sued.
It would mean :
That I do not believe in my work,
and in what I write.

So, that's not gonna be here.
If you want to sue me, go ahead.
But I will give you a guarantee :

If you are not satisfied with my book,

send it back to me.

And I will give you back the money,

that you paid for it.

Guaranteed.

I am primarly a business man,

and I have to do what I say

or write.

Because I have a good reputation

&

want to keep it good.

You should know that I write Nonfiction.

This is a reassurance for you.

Because I earn my money as a

salesperson.

I am not dependant on people buying my books.

And this means, that I don't have to make up

wonderfull stories & make false promises.

I write from my life & business experience.

Just the facts.

To give you the best experience,

there will be a short bio of me,

so that you get to know me a little better.

Then I will tell you how & why

this book came into existence.

Then you get to read the book.

And after that, you get your surprise,

which I included to overdeliver & delight
You.

The bio of author Jasmin Hajro, nice to meet you

Hello dear reader, how are you ?

Thank you for buying one of my books.

My name is Jasmin Hajro,
I was born on July 6, 1985 in Bosnia.
As refugees, we came to the Netherlands 21 years ago.
After having completed school & worked at several jobs ...

On 17 December 2012, I founded my first company:
investment firm Jasko. After a successful first year,
I unfortunately had to close that company.

After a short period of rest, unemployment and temporary work.
I started again as an entrepreneur.

On September 1, 2015, I founded establishment Hajro.

(We say establishment instead of company,
because we do a bit more then just sell stuff.
Like providing jobs,
donating to 40 different charities,
and helping people to live richer.)

Since the beginning the core activity is,
selling sets of greeting cards,
door to door.
Nowadays the product range has been expanded.

With, among other things, the selling of my 12 books.

The royalties of my books are donated to the charity:
foundation Giveth Life.
From there more than 40 other charities
receive donations.
And by buying this book, so do you.
Thank you.

My company is now part of Hajro Group,
which consists of 19 different subsidiaries,
that are part of 1 umbrella organization.
Called Energy Now (Energie Nu)

For more information about my company
& the foundation, go to www.hajrobv.nl

How this book came into existence

In 2007 I started working at a restaurant, as a dishwasher. I lived with my mother and had no living expenses. I earned about 1000,- euro per month. So I had enough money in savings. At my work I learned to work in the kitchen & worked my way up. Then I learned that my saving were not actually growing with the interest, because inflation was as high as my interest.

I did a home course called Wiser with money. Then home course Stock exchanges and investing.
I read books on finance.
Somewhere I learned that for retirement : If you live in a foreign country for a couple of years or are an immigrant

When you retire, you will get a

pension cut.

Because you don't have a complete

employment history of 47 years.

This meant that my parents were

screwed, when they retire.

(Becaues they are immigrants,

and will only have worked in the Netherlands

for about 20 years.)

How would they survive with a half pension ?

When they're old and can't work anymore,

and when they should be enjoying life.

Then I decided to become rich.

I had to, so I can give them a decent pension.

So I went on with educating myself on finance.

Read more book on finance.
Started investing,
in mutual funds, bonds, stocks.
Made some profit & also lost some money.
No problem, I was lerning.

But I was exhausting myself,
because I also worked fulltime in the kitchen.

So I started looking for a better way,
that would cost me less time & energy.

And thru thinking about how to do it better.

I came up with a system.

When I started a company to invest

professionally for clients,

I applied for a patent.

To protect my financial system.

(It's kind out outside the intention of
this book. But If you want to know what
happened. My company Jasko had 1600,- euro
in the portfolio. If I made a 20% return on
that, I could pay the promised return
to my clients, which I did, and buy a
present for myself.
But it was not enough to make a living.
And then I also had no clue about selling,
which is required to get new clients.
And I had to close the company.
Which hurted, because it was my baby.
But I have the experience.)

Now I have received the patent

for my invention

the financial system.

You can see it at the next page.

Rijksdienst voor Ondernemend Nederland

OCTROOINUMMER 1040234

Octrooicentrum Nederland verklaart dat op grond van octrooiaanvraag 1040234, ingediend op 29 mei 2013, octrooi is verleend aan:

Jasmin Hajro te Doetinchem, Nederland.

Uitvinder(s): Jasmin Hajro te Doetinchem, Nederland

Voor: Financieel systeem.

Een recht van voorrang werd ingeroepen, gebaseerd op octrooiaanvraag: 1040030, ingediend op 30/01/2013 in Nederland.

Aan dit bewijs is een exemplaar van het octrooischrift gehecht met nummer 1040234 en dagtekening 14 februari 2018.

De maximale beschermingsduur van dit octrooi loopt tot en met 28 mei 2033.

Uitgereikt te Den Haag, 27 februari 2018

De Directeur van Octrooicentrum Nederland,

mr. D.J. de Groot

Well...

I gave you my bio,

so that you know me a little better.

I have told you how & why

this book came into existence.

And now is the time for you to read

the book.

Remember that I write Doing books,

which means that I describe actions that you

can take and from them get results.

Don't worry, it doesn't take a lot of your

time. And I have kept it simple.

The good news

Money keeps flowing into your life.
Money continues to flow.
Money keeps circulating.
Money has done this for hundreds of years.
Money will continue to do this for hundreds of years.

Since you first received pocket money,
since you were paid for your first job.
Since your studentloan money began to come in,
since your job started paying your monthly salary.
Since your business became profitable.

Money kept flowing into your life every month.

Even to people with social wellfare.
Thank God.
Fortunately money keeps coming in regularly.

There is enough money in the world.
Should it be necessary, than more money will be made.

the Pay Yourself First rule

It means that when you receive your money,
you first pay yourself.
For example by saving 10% of it.

To clarify the result,
we will make an example calculation.

For example, you earn 3000 dollars per month.
And you pay yourself first,
in other words: you save 10% of your income.
That is 300, - dollar per month.

A year has 12 months,
So after 1 year you have
(12 x 300) = 3600, - dollar.
After 1 year you have saved a whole month's salary.

If you save 10% every month,
how much will you have after 10 years?
(3600 x 10) = 36000 dollar.
So after 10 years you'll have 36000 dollars
or a whole year's salary in your savingsaccount.

Later on in this book,
you'll see how to make that money that you save every month.
Grow faster.

10% of everything

It is important that when you first pay yourself,
by saving 10%.
That you save 10% of everything.

Of course 10% of your income.

But also 10% of the tip if you get it,
also 10% of your allowances,
also 10% of your gift money,
also 10% of your 13th month,
also 10% of your bonus,
also 10% of your wage increase,
also 10% of your tax refund,
also 10% of your welcome premium.

From which angle or from whom you receive money,

the first thing you do is pay yourself first.

By saving 10% of it.

the secret of success

The secret of success is Persistence.

If it takes 20 years,
for you to become a millionaire.
If that means that it requires of you
20 years,
of working and saving & investing.
Then you have to Persist 20 years with
working and saving & investing.

And not quitting after 5 years ....

PERSIST until you reach your goal.

The 2nd secret of success is:

WHAT YOU DO WITH YOUR TIME

So do not go watch TV for hours,

but start earning money

&

deal with people who earn a lot of money.

So that you learn from them to earn even more money.

That money will start to work hard for you,

according to this system,

that you are learning.

The person who will make you rich,

the one who will build your Fortune,

is YOU.

Therefore, take good care of yourself.

So you can keep on persisting

for a long time,

until you reach your goal.

Trend

Because people live longer nowadays,
they need money for a longer period of time.

Many people build up income for later,
with dividend paying &
interest-bearing investments.

This will increase the value of those kind
of investments,
over time.

The part of your money
that you are going to invest,
will grow because of this trend.

Bonds explained

If you buy a bond,
you actually lend money to a company or government.
You get interest for this,
which is paid to you annually.

A bond usually costs around a thousand dollar.
Some bonds have a certain duration,
for example 10 years.
If this bond gives 5% interest,
with a duration time of 10 years.
And you buy this bond.

Then you get the upcoming 10 years,
50 dollar in interest each year.
After that 10 years, you get your deposit,
that thousand dollar back.

Some bonds have no duration in years mentioned.
There is a P mentioned, the abbreviation for Perpetual,
which means eternal.
These perpetual bonds pay interest annually,
for eternity.
As long as the organization that issues
them still exists.
That can be hundreds of years.

You buy a bond once,
and get 50 dollar in interest each year,
for the next 50 years or longer.
Without having to do anything else for it!

That's better, is it not?

Preparation

Before you start building your own Fortune,
we must do the preparation first.
The preparation consists of 3 things.

1. Have your will prepared by a notary.

This is not fun, but important.
So that when you're gone,
there are no ambiguities or
misunderstandings.
About what you leave behind and to whom.

2. Make sure you are well insured.

Get the insurances that you need,
and think that you will need.
Such as a term life insurance policy and
a funeral insurance.
So that when you're gone,
your surviving relatives do not get stuck
with those costs.
And still have to arrange things.
But that everything is already well
arranged.
Try to get all your insurance policies from
1 or 2 providers, so that you get a discount
on your insurance package.

3. Open the following 3 accounts:

1 A savings account,
2 a deposit account,
3 an investment account.

**(Note : with deposit account is meant a bankingaccount on which you can fix an savingsamount of money,
for 1 to 20 years.
Which pays you interest annually,
and gives back your savingsamount,
after the duration period ends,
which you pick. If you want your savingsamount back before duration ends,
you get a fine.)**

Systematically building it up

You will systematically on these 3 accounts,
build your Own Fortune.
With the amount of your income,
that you save every month.

If you, like in our previous example,
save per month 300 dollar.
Then you divide that 300 dollar,
about your 3 bankingaccounts.
1/3 Saving, so you put 100 dollar in your
savings account.
1/3 Deposit, so you put 100 dollar in your
deposit account.
1/3 Investing, so you put 100 dollar in
your investment account.

Half of your investment account money, you
invest in a dividend yielding mutual fund.
And the other half you invest in an interest
yielding bonds mutual fund.

For example :

50 dollar in the NN Utilities Fund Dis
50 dollar in the Triodos Sustainable Bond
Fund

You can leave it that way, all year round.
Without having to worry about it.

After that year, you will receive interest
from your savings account.
And interest from your deposit account.
And dividend & interest from your investment
account.

This money works for you now.
That's how you let it grow.
You also get over the years,
the interest on interest effect.
Which makes it grow faster.

Every month

Next month you pay yourself first,
by saving 10% of your income.

This amount of 300 dollar you divide again
over your 3 bankingaccounts.
1/3 Saving, so 100 dollar into your savings
account.
1/3 Deposit, so 100 dollar into your
deposit account.
1/3 Investing, so 100 dollar into your
investment account.

Half of your investment account money,
you invest in a dividend yielding real
estate mutual fund.
The other half you invest in an interest
yielding bonds mutual fund.

For example :

50 dollar in the BNP High Income Property
Fund
50 dollar in the NN Global Bond Fund

In total you have:

200 dollar in your Savings account.
200 dollar in your Deposit account.
200 dollar in your investment account
The money in your investment account is
equally divided over 4 mutual funds.

This means for you,
that you receive annual interest on your
savings account.
And that you receive annual interest on your
deposit account.
And that your receive annual dividend &
interest on your investment account.

Every year.

The next month you do the same 3 steps again

Step 1: You save 10% of your income.

Step 2: That 10%, in our example that 300 dollar, you divide over your 3 accounts.
A third into your savings account.
A third into your deposit account.
And a third into your investment account.

Step 3: The amount that goes into your investment account,
you divide in two.
One half you invest in a dividend yielding mutual fund
or
a dividend yielding real estate mutual fund.
The other half you invest in an interest yielding bonds mutual fund.

The next month you do the same 3 steps again.

Then you do the same 3 steps each month.

Why not put everything in your investingaccount?

It is very important that you,
stick to the described dividing.
With this dividing you only risk
a third of your money.

But by having that part that you risk,
spread well.
You reduce the risk.

Mutual funds are already spread in
themselves.
A mutual fund is invested in 50, 100 or
more companies.

Which reduces your risk dramatically.

The amount with which you pay yourself first
every month,
that 10% that you save.
Always divide it into your 3 accounts as
below:
1/3 of that 10% in savingsaccount
1/3 of that 10% in depositaccount
1/3 of that 10% in investingaccount

It is wise to also, divide your investments
in mutual funds
by category,
as below :

1/3 stocks mutual funds
1/3 bonds mutual funds
1/3 real estate mutual funds

Choose mutual funds that pay you dividends
or interest.

It depends

It could be,
that your savings account pays the interest
per month.
Or per year.
That differs per bank and savings account.

It could be that your mutual funds
pay out the dividend per quarter.
Or per year.
That differs per mutual fund.

If you open a deposit account at Rabobank,
the so-called Target Savings.
Then you can decide for yourself,
how often you put money into it,
and how much.
That is a very convenient deposit account.

It may be that other banks,
request a minimum deposit for a
deposit account.
For example 500 dollar.

If the bank where you open your deposit
account,
requires a minimum deposit .
Then you can save that up monthly,
until you have enough to meet the minimum
requirement and put it in a deposit. For
several years.

In our example,
you have after 5 months (5 x 100) =
500 dollar,
saved up.
You then meet the minimum requirement for a
depositaccount.
And you can put 500 dollar in your
depositaccount,
fixed for 10 years or more.

<u>**After 1 year**</u>

After 1 year you saved in total
3600 dollar.
(12 months x 300 = 3600 dollar)

You have done the 3 steps on a monthly basis.

Now you have:

1/3 of 3600 is 1200 dollar and that is in your savings account.
1/3 of 3600 is 1200 dollar and that is in your deposit account.
1/3 of 3600 is 1200 dollar and that is in your investment account.

You have spread your investments in mutual funds per category,
So :

1/3 of 1200 is 400 dollar and that is in stocks mutual funds.
1/3 of 1200 is 400 dollar euro and that is in bond mutual funds.
1/3 of 1200 is 400 dollar and that is in real estate mutual funds.

You have invested in mutual funds that pay out dividend and interest, to you.

So you receive interest and dividend on your investment account.
You will receive interest on your deposit account.
And you also receive interest on your savings account.

Step 4 and 5

Step 4: If you have 1200 dollar in mutual funds, you sell 1100 of it.

In our example, you have invested 1200 dollar every year in mutual funds.

So every year you sell 1100 dollar from your mutual funds.

So that you have 1100 dollar in cash, on your investment account.

Step 5: With that 1100 dollar cash on your investment account, you buy 1 individual bond.

A bond that pays a high interest rate to you, and has a long duration time.

Or a perpetual bond that pays a high interest to you.

**Note : It is forbidden for you to buy junk bonds !
Corporate and government bonds are allowed.**

Na 10 jaar

If you do the described steps,
every month and every year.
The next 10 years.

Then you will have :

1200 x 10 years = 12000 dollar on your savings account.
1200 x 10 years = 12000 dollar on your deposit account.
1200 x 10 years = 12000 dollar on your investing account.

Every time you had 1200 dollar
in mutual funds,
you sold 1100 dollars of it.
And from that cash you bought 1 bond.
So after 10 years you have 10 bonds.

If you have bought perpetual bonds,
that pay 10% interest per year,
You receive (10 x 100) = 1000 dollar in interest annually.

Well then you can buy 2 bonds per year.
From what you save and divide into your investingaccount
& from the interest payout from your bonds.

This will result in increasing your total annual receivable rturns.

Increasingly bigger annual returns for you

In the course of time, your total returns annually,
increase by the interest & dividend that you receive.
This allows you to buy more and more bonds per year.
And thus, your total annual returns become even bigger.

For example after many years:

You have 10 perpetual bonds that pay 10% interest annually,
you receive 1000 dollar per year in interest.
And you have 100 bonds that have a duration time of 20 years,
which payout 8% interest.
You then receive 8000 dollar per year in interest.

Plus the interest that you receive on your savings account
& plus the interest that you receive on your deposit account.

In total, your annual returns are more than ten thousand dollars.

And with that you can buy more individual

           bonds,
so that your total annual returns
         become even bigger.

             In this way,
  the system is reinforcing itself,
to yield bigger annual returns for you,
             every year,
       for the rest of your life.

What now & how do you proceed ?

If you understand this book,
and you understand all the steps
that you have to do.
If you are going to do everything yourself,
then that's fine.

Get started.

Start building your Fortune.

If you think you can use some help,
you can ask that someone.
You can ask your adviser at the bank.
Or you find an independent consultant.
Then you can together
Build your Fortune.

———————

Put this book in a place,
so that you see it every day.
So that it reminds you of your goal:

Building your own Fortune.

And so it reminds you of the steps you have
to do every month & every year.

———————————————

Thank you for buying this book

&

good luck with

Building Your Fortune.

P.S. I recommend that you reread this book
every month. To stay focused.

If you like this book and get good value
from it,
please be so kind to recommend it
to the people that you know.

Or sent a copy or 2 as a gift.

So that it helps them to

improve their lives also.

Thank you.

Kind regards,

Met vriendelijke groeten,

Jasmin Hajro

Hajro
Ottawastraat 19
7007 BC
Doetinchem,
the Netherlands
KvK : 65686306

www.hajrobv.nl

Ok,

thank you very much for placing your trust in me.

I have promised you a surprise.

It's yours

on the following pages.

I hope that when you have finished

reading the entire book,

that I have delighted you

with the surprise.

Enjoy.

Book Victory

Hello again...

I am Jasmin Hajro,
and you just have read a few things about me
in my bio.

But you have bought this book because you
want to know the whole story.

My life story ....

I called it Victory,
because I have overcome a few things.

I am 32 years old and live in Doetinchem,
in the Netherlands.
I work as a salesman
on behalf of Hajro.
I sell sets of greeting cards,
gift mugs and booklets.

Part of the proceeds go to more than 40 Charities.

You can find everything about establishment Hajro at
www.hajrobv.nl

I now live in the Netherlands.

But on 6 July 1985 I was born in Sarajevo,
in Bosnia.

When I was a young child, we lived in Gora.
That is a village in Bosnia.
It is on a mountain.
A mountain village.

The view is great,
lots of nature.
Clean, fresh air.

I remember it as a happy time.

The house we lived in
was a kind of 2 houses under 1 roof.
Aunt Rahima had lived in the other part.
Until her own house was built.

My parents both worked,
and I went to Biba,

an elderly woman in the village,

that was my babysitter.

I remember she had an old-fashioned stove,

which worked on firewood.

And we placed unripe walnuts

behind the stove, to ripe.

Under our house,

you had a steep part of soil,

and below that a flat piece of land.

On that flat piece of land,

we grew vegetables,

potatoes and very small tomatoes.

There were also pear trees and walnut trees growing there.

My mother worked at Tas,

an automobile factory,

where they made or processed.

small car parts.

I do not remember anymore
what kind of work my father did then ...
You notice that it has been a very long time ago.
I was always very happy to see him,
when he came home.
And asked once if he could work 2 days a week,
and be free 5 days a week.

My uncle Ibro lived close to us,
with Aunt Sevda and my nieces :
Sanela and Amela.
They had a red swing.
I have been swinging on it and went
as high as possible,
Until I got a kind of butterflies in my stomach feeling,
by excitement.
I do not know how to exactly describe that feeling.

With my cousins I did play games such as hide & seek.

I once wrestled with my father
and then I ended up falling weird on my wrist,
it hurted.

Then Dad said: hajmo kod Ibre rostiljat

Let's go barbequing at Uncle Ibro.

I went to the mosque,
and learned prayers
and how to pray.

I asked the hodza
that's a kind of reverend,
how you can know if someone is lying.
He said you can see it on the forehead.
That it turns a little red.

It is very peaceful in the mosque,
I still see it that way.
Although it has been a while since I visited one.

———

It is now March 27, 2018,
00:44 hours at night.

I'm getting out of bed in the mornings, late again....

I wake up at 9 or 10 in the morning
from the alarm clock.

I then switch off the alarm.
And fall asleep again.
When I wake up again afterwards it is already noon.

I had sleeping pills a few weeks ago,
for 2 weeks..
It went well
I started going to bed earlier,
and getting up earlier. Before noon.

Maybe it is a strange time, in the middle of the night
to write a book.
But I thought that once, I just had to start writing it.

When I was playing at Chess Club Doetinchem,
I said to Frans that I wanted to write a book
about my life.
That could have been in 2009.

———————

Biba, the woman who looked after me when my parents worked,
was also the babysitter of an orphan.
I do not remember what his name was.
But we went to the mosque together.
There he farted ...
And we were both thrown out.

My father drove a Fico,
that is like a kind of old model Fiat 500 car.
If we drove to Grandpa and Grandma,
I could sit on Dad lap
behind the wheel.

The first time I saw snow,
I walked outside in my pajamas.
I was completely stunned to look at it.
Amazing.
It must have been cold outside.
The winters in Bosnia are colder than here.

My father became very angry,
and I got a beating with his belt.

I remember that I was rolling over the ground
and called: nemoj babo
Don't hit me, Dad

My index finger was completely swollen,
because I was hit there too.

I still love it
to look outside
when it snows.
Everything seems so peaceful then.

Oh, those beatings were normal.
That was how you got punishment,
and how other children received punishment
in Bosnia.

I was 6 years old when I went to school for the first time.

When my sister, Emina was born and I saw her for the first time,
she looked tinted. And I thought she was not my sister.

My father once had in an angry mood,
thrown the TV out of the window.
I have around my twentieth year
done the same thing once.

Once my father went to Aunt Rahima,
and I was not allowed to go with him.
Then I went outside
and looked in through the window at them.
My father got angry,
and I had to sit naked in front of the house.
If I wanted a beating,
then I could ask
my daddy, he told me.

My father drank,
mom says he beat her too.

The war had started
between Bosnia and Serbia.

We had moved
because the enemies came too close.
We have moved a number of times.

My father had to fight for Bosnia,
in the battlefield. And was not always with us.

We left the village
and we were in an abandoned house.
I do not remember what that place is called.
We have harvested grain,
and grown potatoes.
We took care of the cow of uncle Ibro,
Galava.

On my fathers request, I had tied Galava to a tree,
so she could graze grass.
But I hadn't shortened the chain
and she had too much
walking space

so she had eaten a number of our potato plants.
I got another beating.

You could hear the shooting from a distance.
A house near the one where we were in, was blown up.
We left that place in the evening.

A previous hotel became at that time
a shelter for refugees.
We spent a while there,
and got food packages.
I also fell on the stairs there
with a bottle of milk,
and had a cut on my wrist.
It is been stitched and the scar
looks like a cross.
You can still see it,
on my left hand.

My father was not with us
in that shelter.

I remember that we were waiting one time,
with lots of people,
probably for those foodpackets.
It was so oppressive ...I felt like I was choking.

My aunt Rahima had already fled to the Netherlands,
and they arranged that we could go there too.

I remember that I had to hold my sister's hand
and was not allowed to let go. When we were with the cow
walking through the forest.
I do not know how long we have walked.

My father stayed behind at a border.
And said to mom
prepare today for tomorrow &
prepare tomorrow for the day after tomorrow

We had help from a woman in Croatie.

Eventually we were awaited somewhere
by Aunt Rahima.

We signed in as refugees.
And went to an asylum seekers center,
a period of time in Alkmaar ..
And a period of time in Kampen near Dronten.

There, I watched Lion King for the first time and
almost had to cry,
because I missed my father.

We went to school and learned Dutch.

After the asylum seekers' centers we got a Roahuis
in Doetinchem,
on the Leliestraat. (lilystreet)
(a Roa house meant that we had a house and
the government paid the costs for living,
if I remember correctly)

After 5 years we received the Dutch nationality.

It was a red appartmentbuilding on the Leliestraat,
where we lived.
We got to know Zihra,
who lived in the blue building.
Also from Yugoslavia.

There were 3 brothers in our red flat,
a few houses further.
One of them had hanged himself.

My father came to the Netherlands wounded.
We had those piggy banks,
in which we saved money.
So that dad could come to us.

It would be like before,
our family together .....

I played a fighting game with Dad on the Nintendo.
And he made baked eggs in the morning.
Very tasty.

The reunification did not last long.

My father left us.
My parents then divorced.

We got a rental house in Doetinchem,
at the Ottawastreet 19.

We are still living there now.
Although mom now has a boyfriend,
and is with him in the weekends.
And my sister Emina,
is now very pregnant.
I will be an uncle,
in a few weeks.

I once already had described on paper
this piece of my life :
my time in Bosnia and
the flight to the Netherlands.
And called it Rebel.
With more details,
but I lost it.
Or someone took it.

After group 8 I went to the MAVO.
At the Rietveld lyceum in Doetinchem.
I obtained the Mavo diploma.

The Mavo lasts 4 years,
I think in the 3rd year
of the Mavo,
I had moved and lived with my father for a while.
In Smilde, province of Drenthe.

Then I came back to mom.
Heartbroken.

———————————————

I think this will become a series ......

Are you looking forward to the sequel?

To be continued.

" By the way, I started my first company in 2012.

I have made more than 700 sales since

1 September 2015 so far.

So I have a track record
in sales and business,
and I know what I'm talking about. "

"" As you have probably already understood,
I earn my money by selling for my own company.
That's my work.

The proceeds from my books go to charity.

I write from experience,
I write to help people move forward
in their lives and business "

book The Ultimate Winning Strategy for entrepreneurs

How do we measure success in business?
With monetary points, with earned euro's or dollars.

What is a successful business?

Successful entrepreneurship =
selling a lot

We are therefore successfully running our business,
if we sell a lot.

So success in doing business = selling a lot
(many sales realized / many sales closed)

Because sales means profits.

So what is the Ultimate Winning Strategy in business?

First we start with the concept,
then you get 2 examples from real life

Have you noticed that supermarkets are open 7 days a week?

Supermarkets may be a less good example,
because we just have to eat and drink.

Have you been to the Esso gas station?
(Part of Exxon mobil corporation)
The Esso gas station has a shop with staff,
and is open 24 hours a day, 7 days a week.

And no, even if it seems that we need petrol,
the Esso could also have become a self-service gas station,
where you fill your tank and pay with a creditcard.

But the Esso has a shop with staff, 24/7 .

What do the supermarkets do every day?

<u>They make sales and profits.</u>
<u>Every day !</u>

What does the Esso do every day and night?

The Esso makes sales day and night,
every day.
<u>So the Esso makes profits,</u>
<u>every day and night of the year</u>

The supermarkets and the Esso are successful
because they realize sales every day
and thus make profits every day.

The Ultimate Winning Strategy for entrepreneurs
is
making profits every day.

Make a profit every day of the year.

You do that by selling every day,
and by daily closing sales.

Your advantage over your competition

If you sell every day & make profits every day, do you than have an advantage over companies who only make profits 5 days a week?

Example 1 from real life

I have been selling from Monday, September 18, 2017
untill Wednesday, September 27, 2017,
10 days in a row,
and made 22 sales in total.

So every day I made sales & I made profits everyday.

That is the Ultimate Winning Strategy for entrepreneurs in action.
(in the real life of running your business)

Well if we are honest,
then we know that the transaction value
of sets of greeting cards is modest.
And therefore the profit per sale is also.

But do not be turned off by those numbers ...
You will soon receive a real life example from someone who
made 1 million.

This was to make you understand the successful Concept
of the Ultimate Winning Strategy for entrepreneurs
and that you see proven that it works.

You now understand that Concept,
you have seen some examples of companies
applying the Ultimate Winning Strategy.
You have seen a real life example
from me I have proven to you that it works.

And you are 100% assured that the Ultimate Winning Strategy works.

People do not need greeting cards
like they need food and drinks,
but they bought every day
and I made profits every day.

So it does not matter what kind of product or service you sell.

<u>The Ultimate Winning Strategy also works for you.</u>

Next step

You understand the Ultimate Winning Strategy for entrepreneurs,
and you know it works.

So now you are going to do it.

You are going to implement it.

I'm not asking you to work 7 days a week,
although you should do it once.
(That will boost your confidence)

You can sell from Monday to Friday &
hire someone who sells for you
from Saturday to Monday (a part-timer)

Then you will already have
sales every day and profits every day.

If I can do it alone,
then you can certainly do it with 2 people!

Are there any other ways how you can
make sales everyday & profits ever day?

Consider, think and find 20 ways,
with which you can make sales everyday

and therefore make profits everyday.

Write them down.

1 Hire a salesperson
2 Create a team of salespeople
3
4
5
6
7
8
9
10
11
12
13
14
15
16
17
18
19
20

Example 2 from real life

Go to www.youtube.nl
and watch the video of Walter Bergeron,
GKIC marketer of the year.

The video lasts about half an hour.

Pay close attention when he says: that means also on saturdays
and sundays.

(that he was selling 7 days a week and
making profits every day)

Have you seen
what the Ultimate Winning Strategy for entrepreneurs
can do for you?

Go to work,
go out selling every day & making profits every day.

Apply your 20 ways,
give your sales a boost,
make lots of profits.
Every day of the year.

I wish you a lot of succes.

P.S. If you have liked this book and got good value from it,
than would you be so kind
to recommend it to people that you know.
So that it also helps them forward.
Thank you.

Book Overcoming tough times

What are tough times?
Isn't that different for everyone?

Perhaps something like tiring times.

Times that make you tired.

I worked in a tapas restaurant in Arnhem,
called Ramblas.
The food was delicious,
but I waanted to do something else,
then work in the dishes and the kitchen.

I started a home study for Wft basic Advisor,
when I worked in that restaurant.
In the evening at home I heard that my uncle Ibro,
who lives in Bosnia, had died.

Things were finally going the right way.
I finally had work and earned money,
could pay my bills.
And reduce my debts.

Well then thas bad news came.

It was as if all energy went out of me.

I have very happy memories of
my childhood in Bosnia.

My family is part of my happy memories.

Someone once asked me what I was missing?
Because I had almost no contact with my uncle.

Apparently, those things go like that,
contacts & connections fade ....
Especially if you live far away from each other.

What I missed was his humor,
it always feels good and joyous when I was there.
And going to Bosnia on vacation is no longer
the same, because the people you go for
no longer exist.

I have thought about it...
Because I have already written 11 books.
The one you are reading now is the first part of my new series:
Work to shine.

What kind of book would be good for many people?
What kind of book would be helpful to many people?

What should be in it, what would it have to give to readers?

Even if it is only recognition,
periods I went through &
that they are going through.
That they can relate to.
To know that you can get through anything.
No matter how painful it is
and no matter how bad it seems, at the moment.

Or comfort.

Maybe relativation,
to attenuate their troubles and their situation &
see them in the right perspective.
They're just like a threshold on the road,
that you really will get over.

To be honest, I do not want to write this book.
I do not feel like writing it.
I really had to force myself ,
to sit down &
start writing.

It is Sunday for God's sake.
July 1st
A new month started,
it is beautiful sunny weather outside.

I got up before noon, for once.

Yeah, for some miraculous reasons,
I am almost 33 years old and I still struggle
to get up in the morning on time.

So what does this Workaholic do?
On such a nice Sunday?

Starting on a new book series &
writing a book that he actually does not want to write.

Well if you've read my book Victory,
then you know that one time in Bosnia
when I was a little boy
I had to sit nude in front of the house. As a punishment.

Because of those kind of fokking things,
I did not really want to write this book.

Anyway,
I have already started ....

So what's in it for you, to know what kind of
extreme punishment I received?

Well, whatever is bothering you,
no matter what kind of tough time you're going through now.
Ans no matter how difficult it may be for you ...

You will never have to sit naked in front of your house,
as a punishment.

You see,
your situation is not that bad.

(That is relativizing, that is to say
relativation or taking the edge off it)

Perhaps there is a better translation ?

But you know what I meant, right ?

Let's go back to Uncle Ibro for a moment,
he left behind a wife and two daughters.

I'm just very sorry that I did not do something for him,
when it was still possible.

I live in a country where I have much more possibilities,
then they have in Bosnia.

I would have liked to send him money every month
And have visited them every year,
or a number of times a year.
Sent them gifts and spent more time with them.

I would have liked him to get to know my great company
& to show him my 11 books which are for sale in 190 countries
worldwide...
And the good foundation that I founded.

But that is not possible anymore,
Uncle Ibro is deceased ....

People of gold

For me that was Grandpa Vejsil and Grandma Ziba.
They too lived in Bosnia.
Grandma and step grandpa actually.

Maybe because they have more experience with parenting,
then my parents.
Or because I never got a beating from them.

It was always great fun with grandpa and grandma.

A lot thanks to her

My father's oldest sister, Aunt Rahima.

Thanks to her, we were able to go to the Netherlands.

To get away from the war.

I owe a lot to her.

In a short period of time

In the period of time, that Uncle Ibro died,
I went to work
& then back home again.

I had enough of it
and I left.

In that period,
that lasted perhaps a half year or 1 year.

Aunt Rahima died of cancer,
Grandma Ziba died.

I went to Bosnia and there
I have carried her coffin for a while.

There was a long line of people and the coffin was passed on.
All the way to the grave.

We had a friend of my mother
in our neighborhood: called Ria.

She drank a little too much and had
a strange fear : she was afraid to walk up the stairs.

It was nice with her, when she came to visit.

She also died of cancer.

In that short period of time.

And then I heard that Grandpa Vejsil
also had died.

A while before, grandmother and grandmother had already split
up.

But still.

That was 5 people in a short period of time.

At that time we received many letters from collection agencies
and bailiffs.
Our bills that they doubled the amounts that we had to pay
and that was all according to the law.

Yah Yah.

They are legitimate thieves.

So I was very angry and sad then.

Very very angry. Warlike angry.

And sad.

As you understand,
I would have liked to have done something more for them.
Spent more time with them.
Have given them more.

And I would loved to show them,
how far I have come.

From being 1 night homeless,
to writing 11 books & publishing them in 190 countries
worldwide
Plus a good foundation &
a company with 16 subsidiaries.

But now it's too late for that.
They are dead.

I stopped using drugs,
after I had taken too much,
and ended up in a coma.

Well if you use yourself or know someone who does that ..
And if you see it as a waste of potential &
want to be clean
or help someone else to become it.

Then it might be good to know,
what I did afterwards.

That was just as important.

I decided, of course, not to do it anymore.
I could not do it anymore.
I think I got an anxiety attack,
when I tried to smoke a blunt.
Because I was shaking,
and wondered if I was going to get a heart attack.

What I did after ...

No more buying that stuff.
Stopped dealing with people who use it.
Yes, I was at home a lot and it was shitty,
but it was better.

I started to become more fanatic with my chess hobby
and kept myself busy with it.

I went for walks.

I thought of people who used as LOSERS

I once collapsed and fell to the ground,
and after that I stopped drinking
alcohol.

What I did after ...
Was not going to the pub anymore.
Didn't go out to clubs anymore.
Drank a lot of tea and coffee.

Went hiking.
I read.
Listened to audiobooks and watched motivational videos
on youtube.

I wrote.

I didn't go anymore to places and people
where alcohol was consumed.

Yes I was a lot of times at home, like a hermit.

But it was better.

Bills and debts

See bills and debts not like a burden,
but as responsibilities.

And people who still have to receive money from you,
are people who trusted you
or have faith in you.

And for that kind of people you are going to make things right.
No matter how much time it takes you.

Put all your bills in 1 folder and put that thing out of sight,
in a drawer or something.

Emplane some cash money around you in your house.

And focus on earning money,
stash money,
and take care of your responsibilities.

Aging sucks

It sucks, right?

Every year, you become a year older.

I thought so too.
And I especially disliked to become 30 years old.
Because I had heard or thought
that after your thirtieth year
you start to decline.
That everything is going to decay and won't function well.

And I thought about, when I become 80 years old,
and nothing functions anymore
to kill myself one way or another.

Until someone said:
The older you get the better it is

And that is the mighty fokking truth,
as far as aging is concerned.

Some children do not even become 10 years old.

Some people don't even become 18 years old.

But you are 30 or 40 or 50 years and having another birthday
& you can live for another year.

How a great gift is that ...
You can do and experience so much. And enjoy.
Be happy
The older you get, the better it is.

The Better thing

Failing and falling on your face is good for you.
And also is rejection.

Because then the Better thing comes on your path.

I had a solution for the banks,
neatly typed out and ready.
They did not want it.

A while after that,
out of my solution I made a book.
book the Lifebuoy for banks
" loyal banking "
(de Reddingsboei voor banken"loyaal bankieren")
The Better thing

I applied for a social wellfare for the 2nd time.
It was rejected.

I walked home,
and then wrote my 3rd book:
book Recipe for Happiness
the Better thing

That is how it will work out for you too.
Do not despair. Work towards your goals and dreams.
The Better thing is coming

a Doing book

Well, as you might already know in the meantime
I write short books.

And Non fiction.
Simply facts and life experiences.

With often things in them that you can do,
or must do.
Actions you can perform,
so that you get results.

You probably already understand that by just
thinking about 10 euros/dollars,
the 10 dollar will not manifest in your pocket.

But if you do something.
Like working for a while.
Then you will receive the 10 dollar.

I would love to recommend to you
my book Recipe for Happiness
(Also a Doing book)

It contains tips and advice that you can easily do &
that help you to have less stress.
To be happier and healthier.

And also help you a bit to overcome difficult times.

Count on one hand

That night on the street is actually the best thing
that has happened to me.

It has put pepper in my ass,
to go to work hard.
And to get more out of myself.

It has also taught me,
that very few people are always there for you.
You can count them on one hand.

Whatever you did,
and however you have behaved.
They are still there for you.

These rare few could be your mom and dad.

Thank them,
appreciate them.

Make some sunshine for them &

make them proud.

Well you now also know with which people you should
spend your time. And not with others.

And that

What I did after I stopped taking drugs and drinking alcohol
was also ...
Working

They were not always the nicest jobs.

But work has really changed my life.

That it will do for you too.

Work is your best friend,
you can always count on it.
You can always 'borrow' money from that friend
after you have worked.

Quote :" Work is the best therapy."
By Doctor Maxwell Maltz

So if you don't believe me, believe the doctor.

Those meager months

And what about those months when you only
earned a few bucks?

I will become a millionaire or die working towards it.

So about really fokking great.

My Victorious series of 10 books &
Another one,
show you:

That if you really want something,
then you can do it too.

No matter what & Whatever they say.

That obvious recipe

It goes something like this:

Write down what you want to achieve in life

Learn, Work & Persist until you realize it

About the same process as getting your driver's license.
Or cooking a meal.
Or getting your diploma.
Or writing a booklet.

Save a part of your money &
donate something to charities.

Keep reading, listening to audiobooks
and developing yourself. Keep growing.

Learn the 80/20 principle,
so that you will only do the most important things,
that give you the most results.

Then you will feel better about yourself &
that also helps you
get thru tough times.

Learn that it does not matter what people say

To achieve the things you want in your life,
the only thing that matters is : what you think and what you DO

If you experience this as a valuable book,
would you please be so kind
to recommend it
to the people that you know.

So that it helps them too with overcoming tough times.

Thank you.

Extra page

After failing with my first company.

I founded a new and better one.

After my burnout, that cost me 2 months of time

I picked myself up, and became active again.

I started working (selling), writing, jogging

and kept going again.

If I can recover & overcome, so can You.

You are designed tougher than

tough times.

I wish for you a lot of strenght &
the best things in life.

Kind regards,
Jasmin Hajro

P.S. If you want to share your experience with my book,
send me a little revieuw or email at
j.hajro@hotmail.com
Thanx.

Small introduction with establishment Hajro

Establishment Hajro is committed to helping the people
in the province of Gelderland,
by providing jobs and keeping people working,
by donating to more than 40 Charities,
and by helping people to live richer.

Today Hajro is a subsidiary of Hajro Group.
The Hajro Group consists of 19 different companies,
who are all part of 1 umbrella organization.
Called Energy Now. (Energie Nu)

We now have several products & services,
and we support more than 40 charities.

Visit us at **www.hajrobv.nl**
and discover what else we can do for you.

Hopefully you will become a raving fan & customer of us.

Book The Recipe for Happiness

A book has been written about a true story ...
About a man who was imprisoned in a
concentration camp at the time of Hitler,
and happy.

So, Happiness has nothing to do with your circumstances.
It has everything to do with,
your choice to be happy,
regardless of circumstances.

Choose to be happy.

Of course there are touhger times in life,
like when someone you love, dies.
That's part of life.
Those times of grief you just have to go through and process.

Processing is best done by talking about it,
to get it off your chest regularly.

Or by writing about it,
if you write down a situation or your feelings about it,
then it's on paper,
and it is less in your head.

Writing is a good outlet.

Processing is also done well by: staying busy.
Whether that is in your work or your hobby.
They say: a rolling stone does not collect moss.
So stay busy ....

Okay, now you have learned a good lesson about how to better
process negative life experiences.

But you're here for the Recipe for Happiness, right?

Well, the lesson you've learned will help
to make the recipe work better for you.

Here it comes then …

You have probably read a local newspaper,
and you regularly check the news.
(the daily news on television)

Have you noticed that about 99% of it is bad news?
Only misery ..
If you did not know better,
you would think that the whole world is going to perish.

If it's a habit for you,
to watch the news every day for half an hour …

Have you ever wondered if it's healthy for you?
Does it make you happy ?
Of course not !

The easiest way to change a habit is by replacing it
with a new habit.

So from today on, instead of watching the worldly news half an
hour a day ………..

Watch COMEDY for half an hour a day.

Mandatory.

Every day.

Well, now at half past eight in the evening it's not news time,
but Comedy time.

If you watch comedy, you relax & you laugh.
Sounds healthier, doesn't it?

Well, laughing every day is easy to do, right?

And replacing your old bad habit in this way,
with a nice, healthy new habit,
is probably easier than you thought.

Except for the fact that relaxation is good for you,
when you laugh, also your body makes endorphins.
Those are natural happiness substances.

Well, after 21 days of daily watching comedy,
you will have formed a new habit.

So watch Comedy every day.

You can watch a lot of standup comedy on Youtube for free.
Simple?
Sure,
but you have to do it,
every day,
until you don't have to think about it anymore,
and you start doing it automatically.

Some Happiness Ingredients in a row:

- Watch comedy every day, at least one hour.

- Eat ice cream, treat someone with an ice cream.

- Work out, throw out your frustration by playing tennis or go for a run.

- Pee in the yard (and if you get a fine for urinating, laugh your ass off)

- Do not worry, life is too short for that (by staying busy, you do not have time to worry)

- Hug the people that you love

- Go enjoy a cup of coffee or tea

- Buy or save a cat or some other pet

- When you receive money, immediately save a part of it

- Don't let the media scare you, the world is not getting worse, the world is getting better.

- Sex, need I say more
(when you have sex your body also
- produces endorphins =
those natural happiness substances)

Maybe the Recipe for Happiness
is different than you had expected....
But that doesn't matter,
the point is that it works &
that it will help you to live happier.

Do it,
it is easier
then looking with a sour face.

If you liked this book & got some value from it.
Would you then be so kind,
please,
to recommend it
to the people that you know.
So that they too can enjoy it
and live happier.
Thank you very much.

It was my pleasure to write and translate
this book (my third one) for you.
I hope it helps you to live happier.
(I know it will, if you do the things it teaches)

And I hope, that we can together make a contribution
to more happiness in the world.
We can.
If you recommend this book and share it.
Then I will promote it.
And together we will make a contribution to
a happier world.

I would appreciate it if you would write a short review.
Thank you for your effort.
Kind regards,
Jasmin Hajro

P.S.S. The surprise was 4 extra books.

I hope you enjoyed them,

and that I delighted you.

P.S. If you want to let me know your experience with my book. Send me a message by email to j.hajro@hotmail.com. Thanx
My Author Website is at
www.jasminhajro6.webnode.nl

You are welcome to visit,
I will give you 10 free ebooks there

See you soon

More books by Jasmin Hajro :

My bibliography....the books that I have written....

(there are more than 43 titles plus the translations plus the boxsets, so I will only name my english titles)

Build Your Fortune

Moneymaker

Recipe For Happiness

the Lifebuoy For Banks "Loyal Banking"

the Ultimate Winning Strategy, for entrepreneurs

(which is for salespeople & businessowners too)

Poems, jokes and book

Victory 1

Victory 2

Always employment & always money in your pocket, everyday.

Things You Don't Want To Know.

Challenges in having your own business, in real life.

how to Grow your money & Build a good retirement in 2 hours per month, for moms, dads, career women and busy people .

Overcoming tough times.

Secrets of writing and selling books.

Double your profits.

Double your profits, extended.

Triumph 1 (boxset)

Triumph 2 (boxset)

Victorious series (boxset)

Through the crisis

Victory 3

My story

My little masterpiece

Victory 4

I don't feel like writing, says the author

Hackers are scouts

Being real and true: in times of fake and pretend

100 % sales rule

Quotes for success

Entrepreneurship course

3

(If you click on them a new window will open, at Lulu, where you learn more about the book

and where you can buy it as paperback or ebook.

If the link doesn't work click here

All my titles are there, but you can search the one that you want..

" I have good experiences ordering at Lulu")

Only available at Amazon and free with Kindle Unlimited are my books :

Lifechanging quotes

the Jasmin Hajro lifestory(which includes Victory 1,2,3,4)

Controversial

This is how you get rich: passively

200 % sales rule

Visit my author website and get 10 free books at

www.jasminhajro6.webnode.nl

Note :

Over the years a few websites have changed….
My author website is now and will always be at
www.jasminhajro6.webnode.nl

You get 10 free books if you visit me there..

My companys website (in dutch) is
www.hajro.be

My companys International website (in english) is :
www.hajro-international.webnode.nl

You are welcome to visit,
maybe there is another great book
or great service for yourself waiting there.

Thank you for choosing one of my books to read.

Hopefully you are willing to rate it 4 or 5 stars and give it a positive review.

Thank you so much

I will continue to sell greetingcards
and write more books
untill retirement,
so more good stuff will be available
at my Author website,
www.jasminhajro6.webnode.nl
make sure that you visit it
every year or
more often than that.

Kind regards,
Jasmin Hajro
P.S. I hope this book helps you to change your life..